Party in a Book
Spots, Dots & Stripes

Rebecca Emberley

two little birds
www.twolittlebirdsbooks.com

In this book you will find hundreds of perforated pieces,
many of them interchangeable, to help you create the perfect DIY party.
(You will probably be able to sweeten up two parties from this book.)
Involve your guests or have it ready and waiting for them.

A passel of 5 year olds? Cocktails for 8? Cat's 12th birthday?
You can do it! No two parties will be the same.

You don't need any special tools or supplies.
You will need: White glue, or tape, maybe some double-sided tape,
scissors (everything is die-cut, but you may want to trim some bits
or use the double-sided sheets for a unique purpose).
String or twine for garlands and tags, and you are good to go.
DIY party goods without the ink cartridges and a little less sweat,
but still plenty of room for your personal touch.

A different color linen or paper napkin will change the look of the party.
Fancy stemware or mason Jars? Picnic table or drinks by the fire?
Beer and cheese or popcorn and lawn games -
it all works with Party in a Book.

I hope you enjoy creating your party as much as I enjoyed
creating these pieces for you!

This book contains pieces to make:

Garlands
Chain garland
Cones for party hats or snack servers
Napkin rings/wraps
Coasters
Cheese papers or tray liners
Gift wrap embellishments
Favor folders
Cupcake toppers
Cupcake wrappers
Tags
Labels - name tags
French fry or snack holder
 and more

Many of these items can be used in multiple ways.
The strips for the chain garland can be used for gift wrap, as
handles for the cones, or to embellish jars and glasses to make
candle holders or lanterns.
The spots and squares can be used to make garlands, seal bags,
top gifts, mark glasses, attach labels, mark food, tag plants, on
chopsticks or to decorate cakes.
The snack holders can be used for cookies, popcorn, veggie
sticks, they all work!
An picture frame makes a perfect tray or just use the papers on a
slab of wood or stone, to serve cheese or appetizers.
The cupcake wraps will also fit a solo cup.
I'm sure there are uses I haven't thought of yet!

Party in a Book with Kids!

For kids, the strips, spots, dots, and squares can be used to make crowns and embellish party hats!
Decorate cakes, cupcakes etc. Make jewelry, create prize ribbons and badges, decorate masks! Create yards of chain garland.
Attach a garland strip to a cone to create a basket. Kids can do it themselves with your help!

Cones

Cones

Reversible double-sided

Roll cone and secure with
glue or tape on tab

Cones

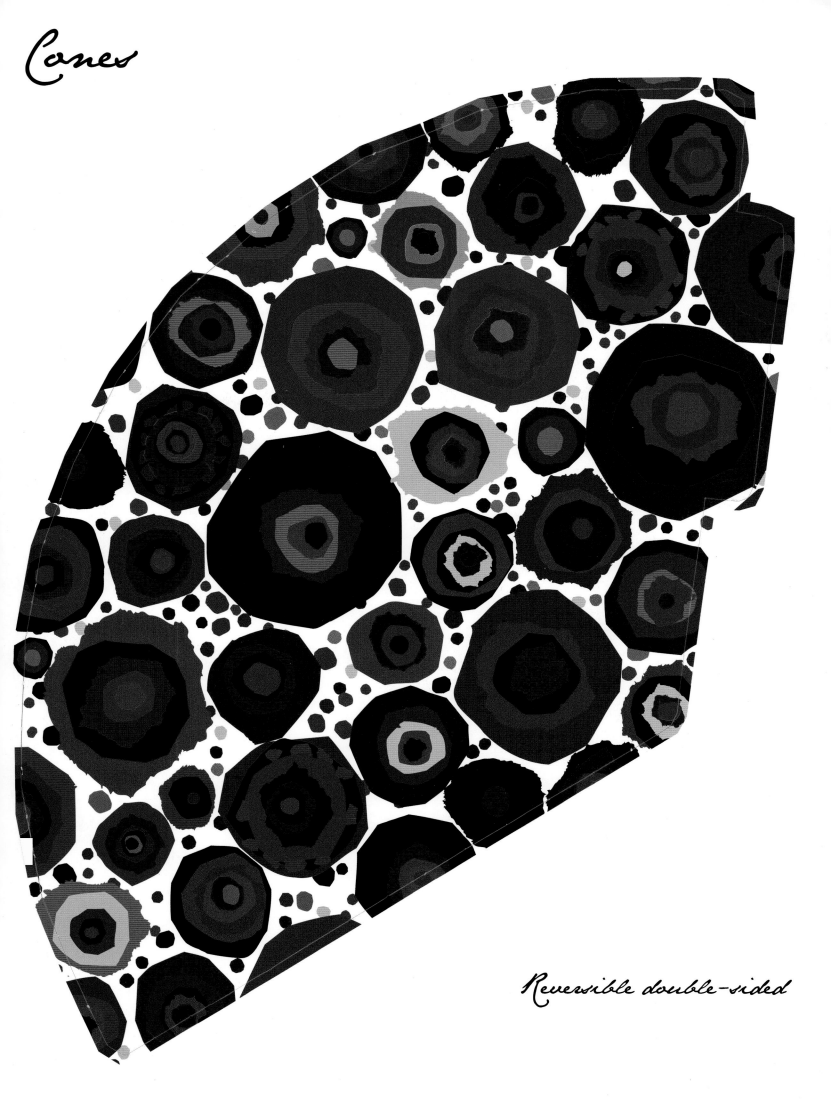

Reversible double-sided

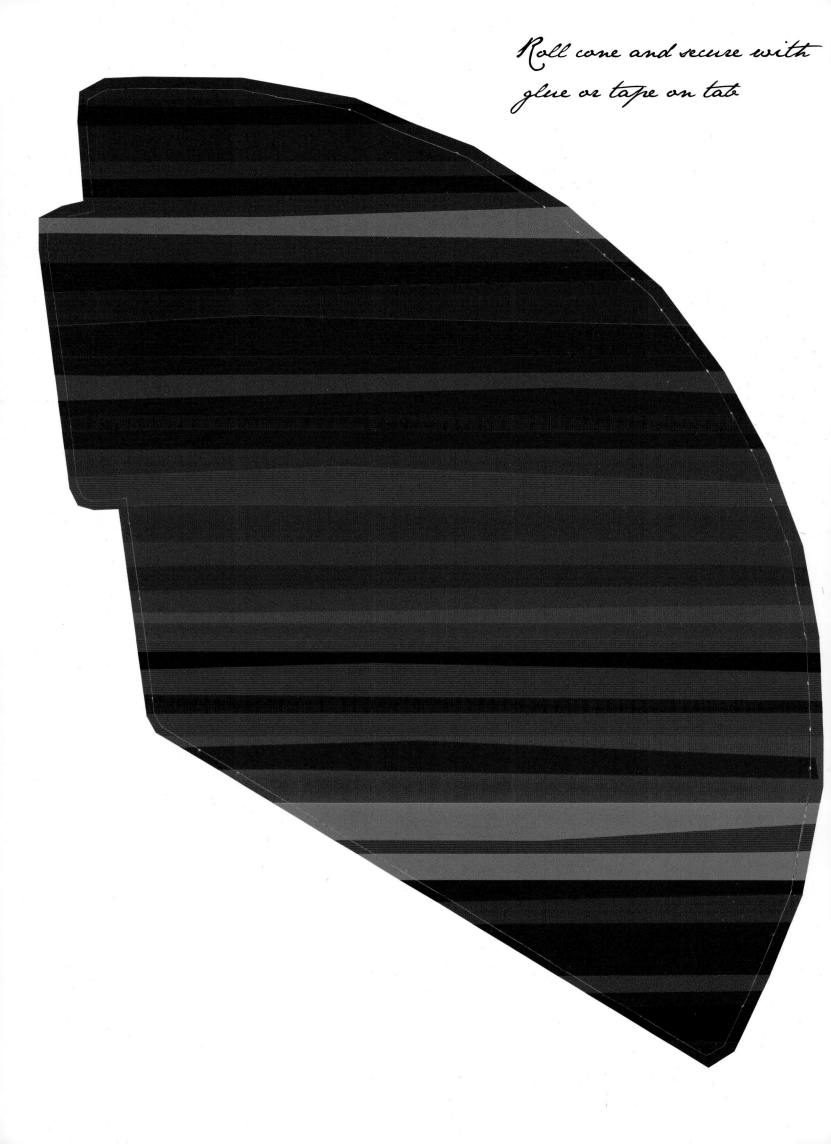

Roll cone and secure with
glue or tape on tab

Cones

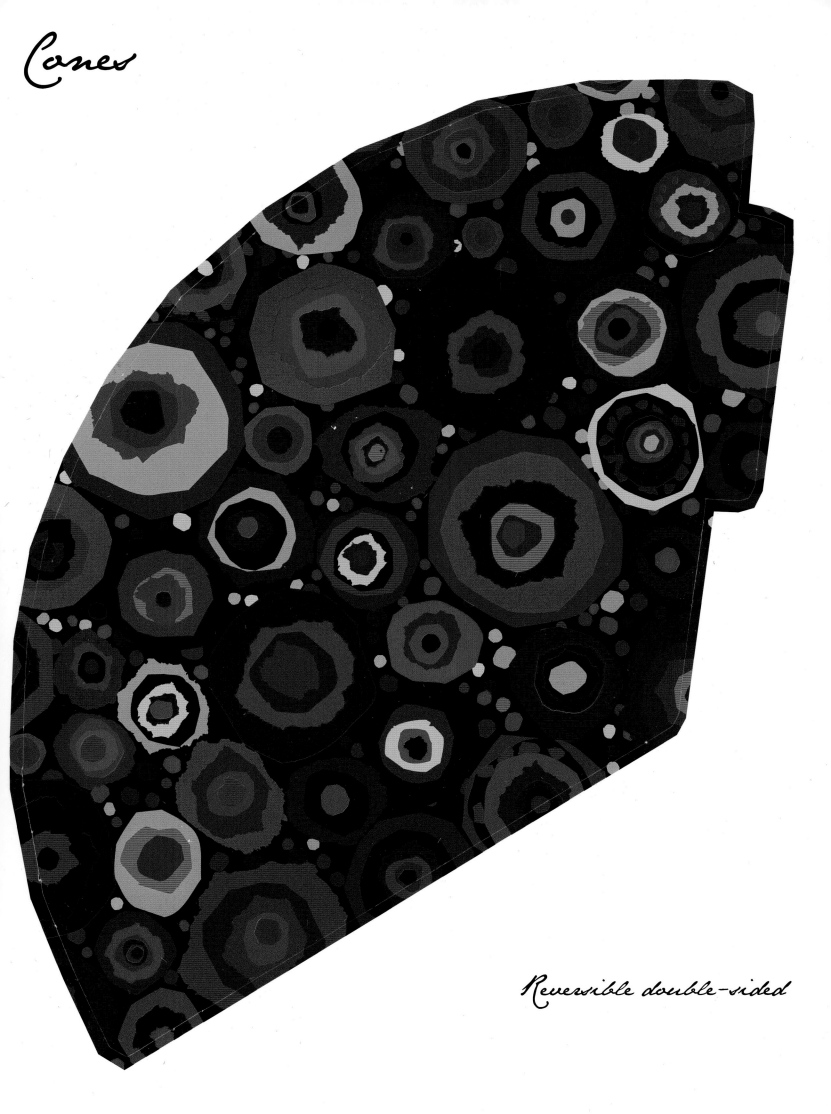

Reversible double-sided

Cones

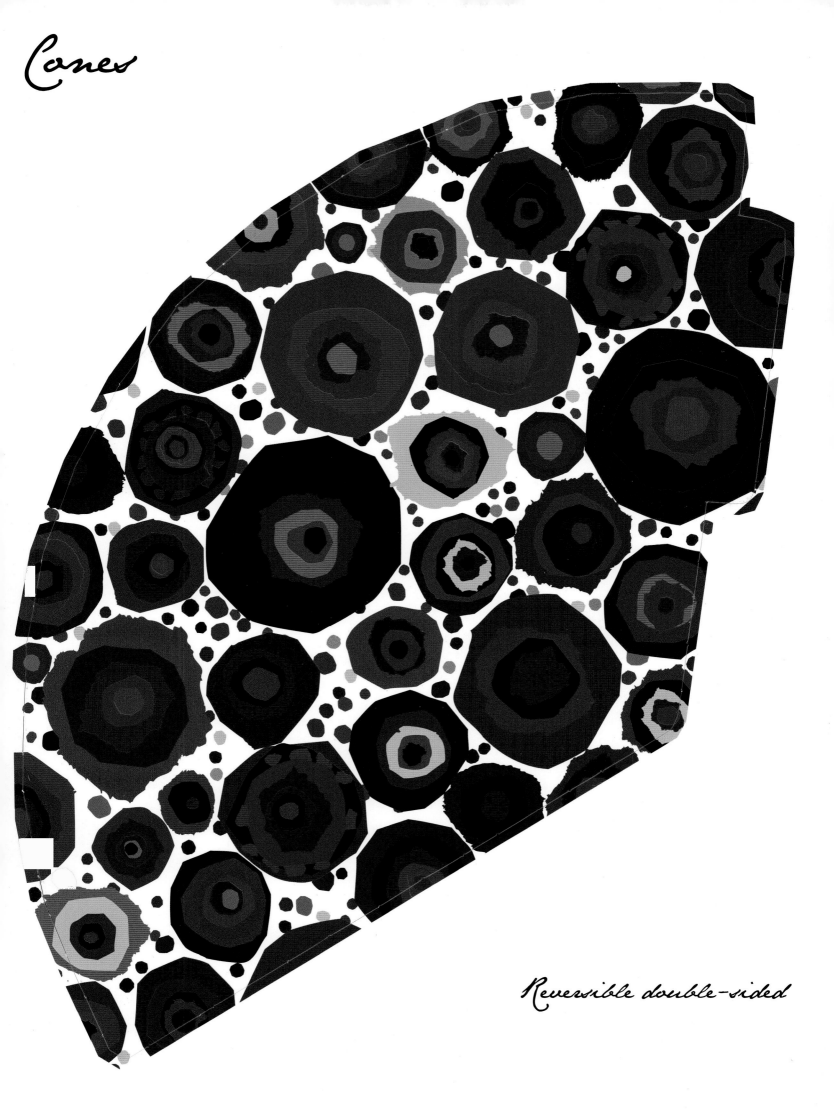

Reversible double-sided

Roll cone and secure with glue or tape on tab

Cones

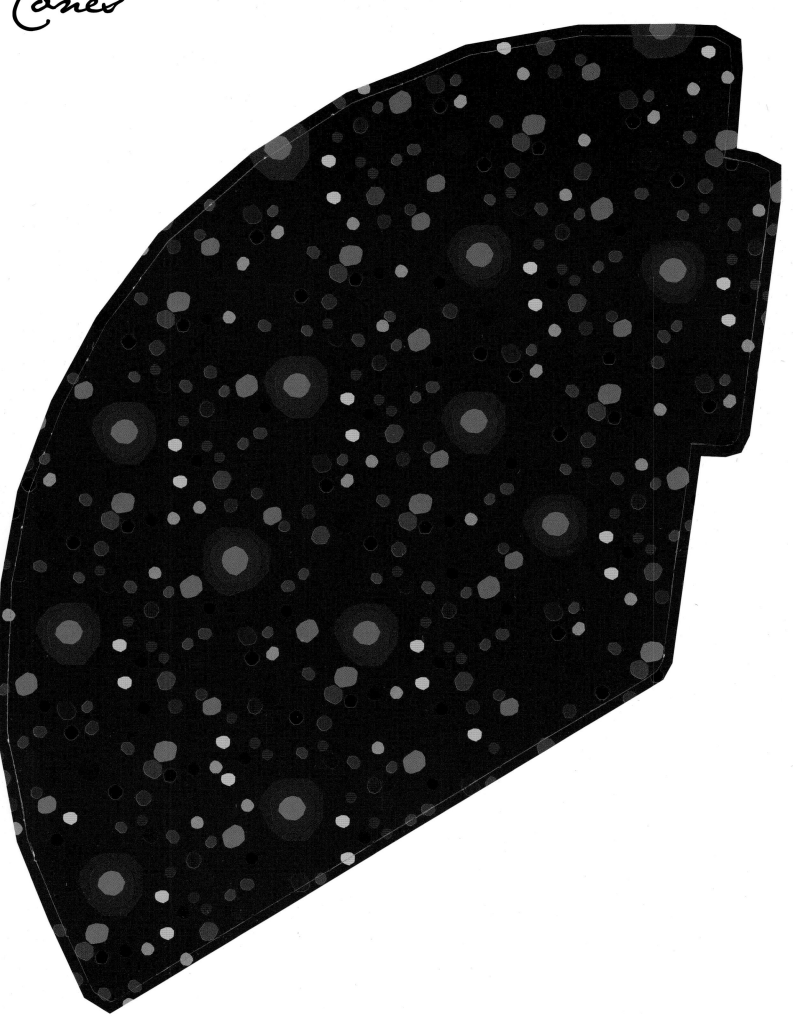

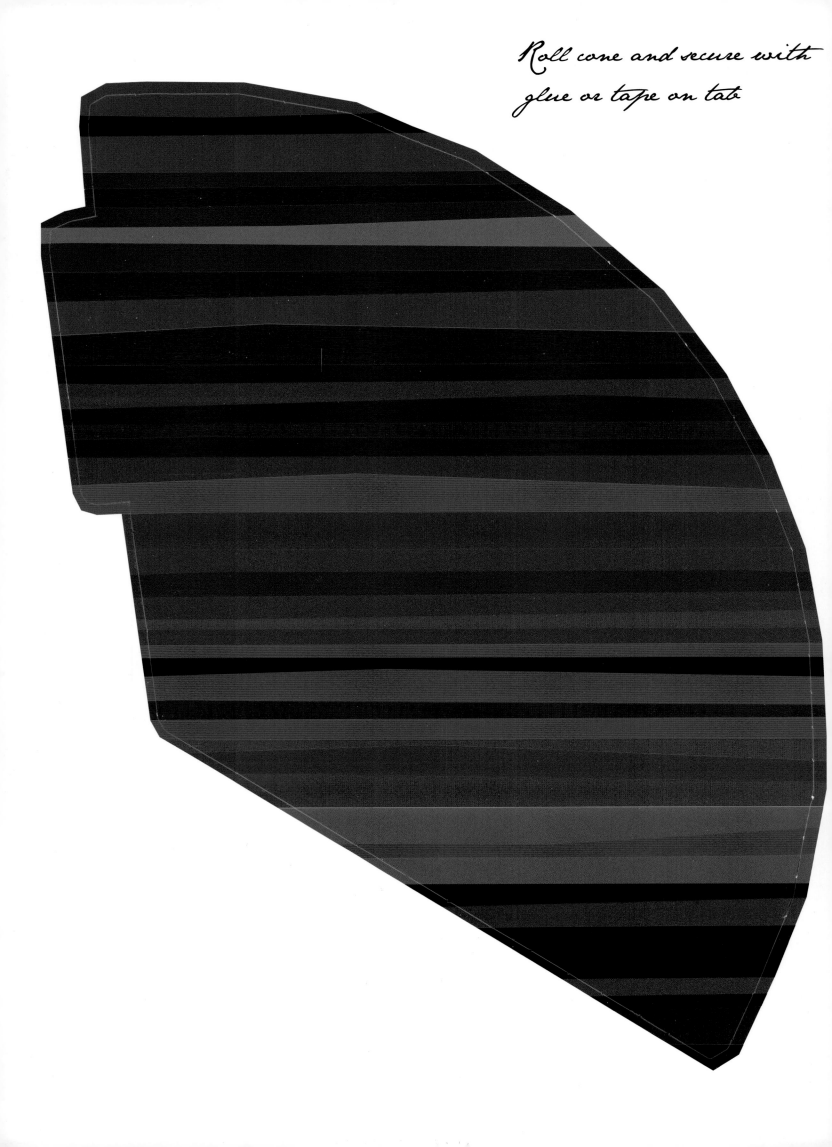

Roll cone and secure with
glue or tape on tab

Cones

Reversible double-sided

Roll cone and secure with glue or tape on tab

Cones

Reversible double-sided

Roll cone and secure with glue or tape on tab

Favor Folderss

Snack Holders

Snack Holders

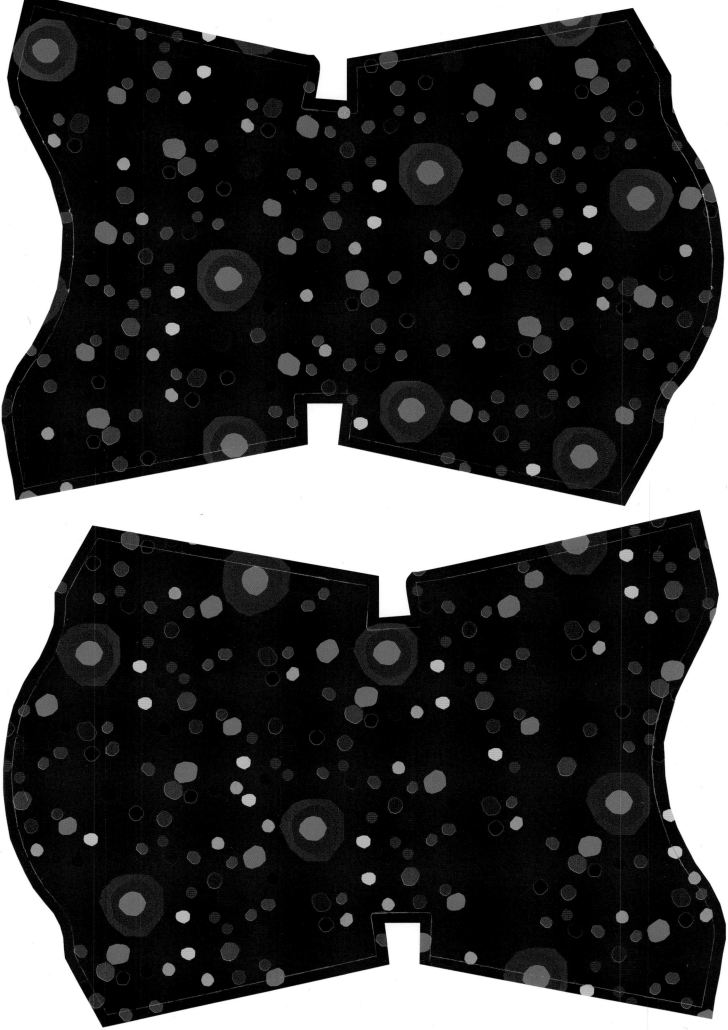

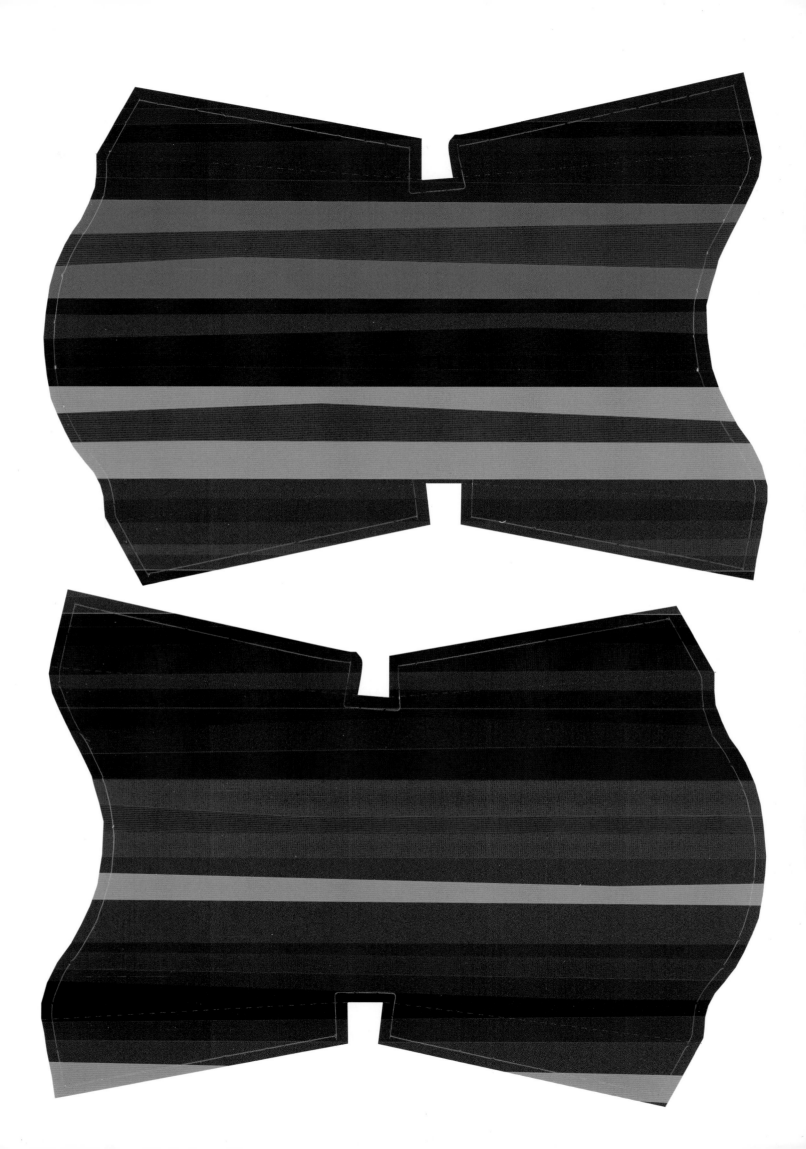

Snack Holders

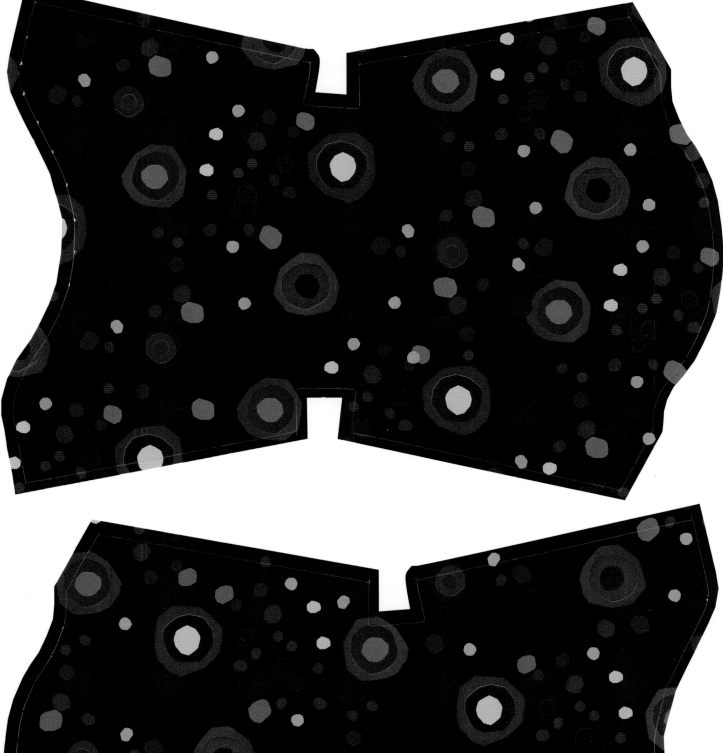

Snack Holders

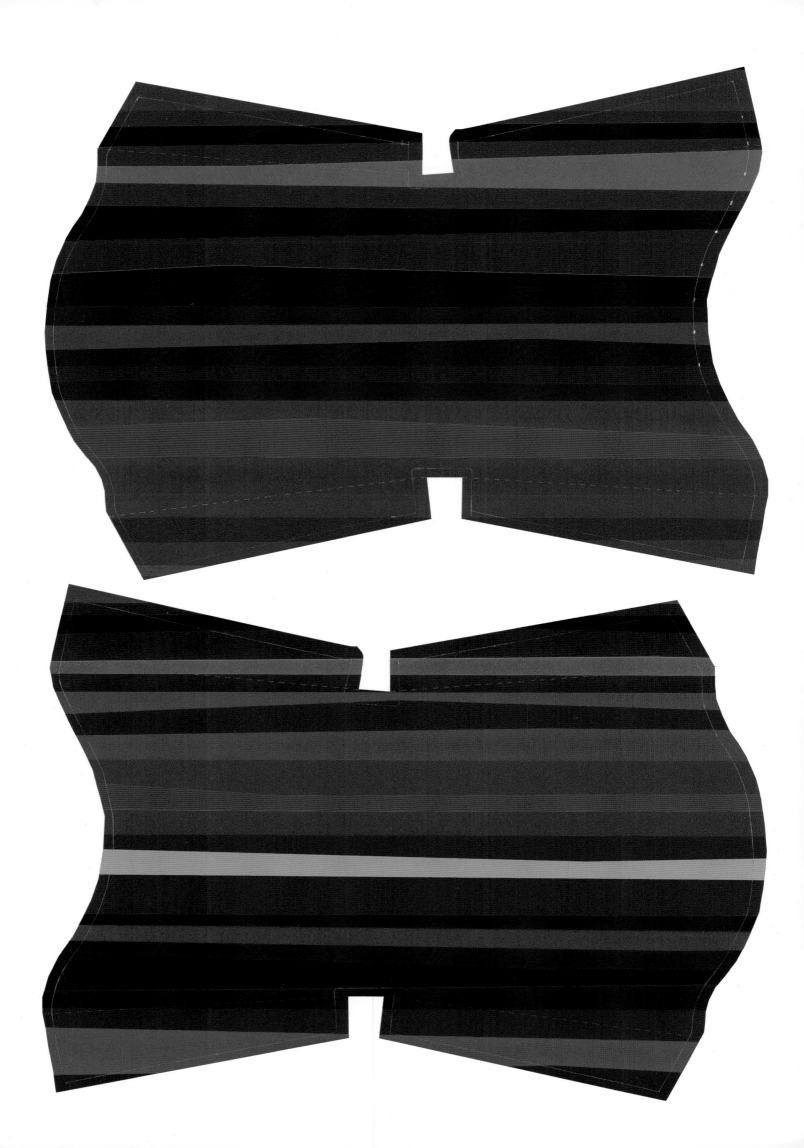

Snack Holders

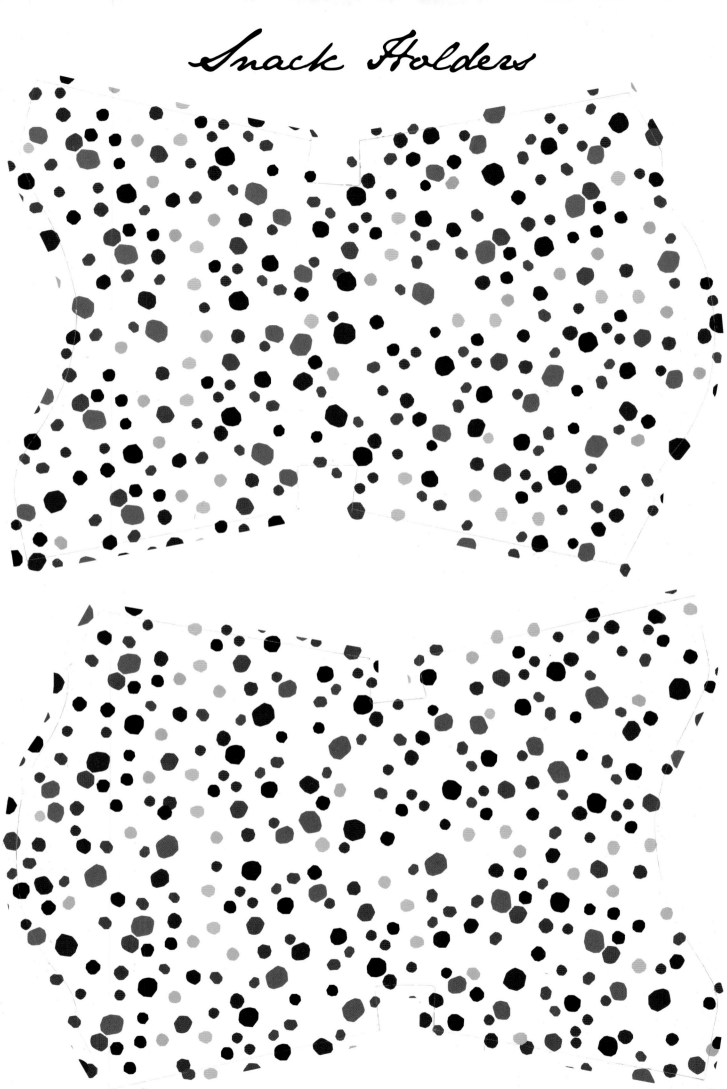

Snack Holders

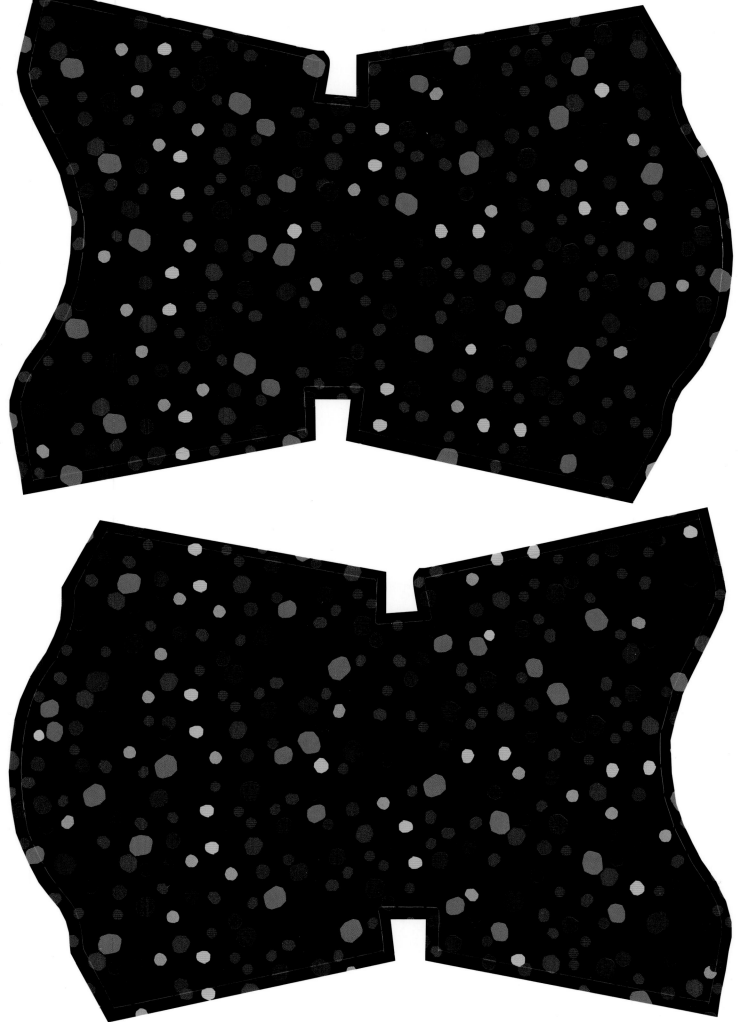

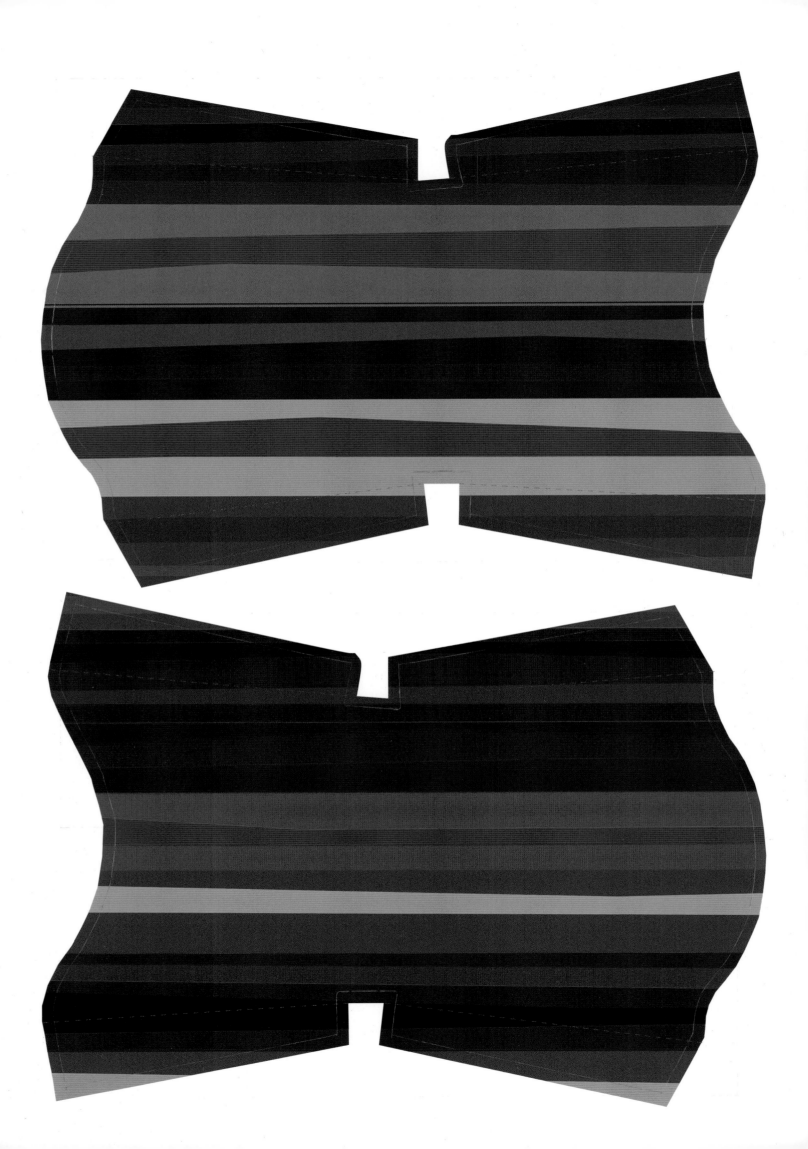

Favor Folders

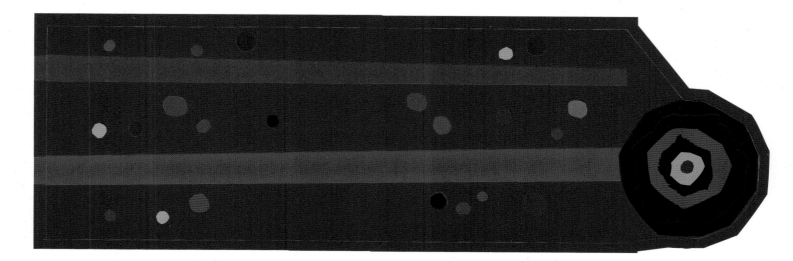

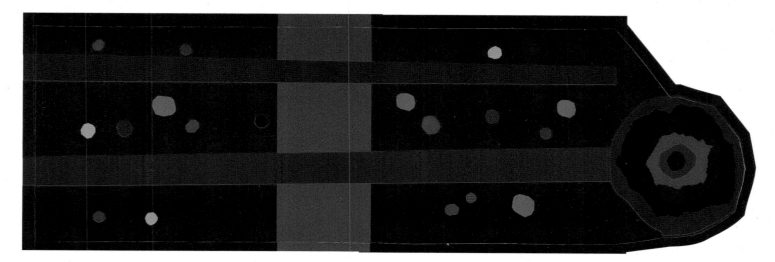

Inside of Favor Folders

Fold over to create top

Fold in to create flat bottom

Favor Folders

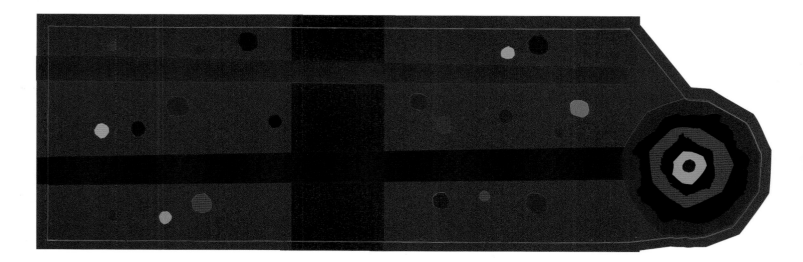

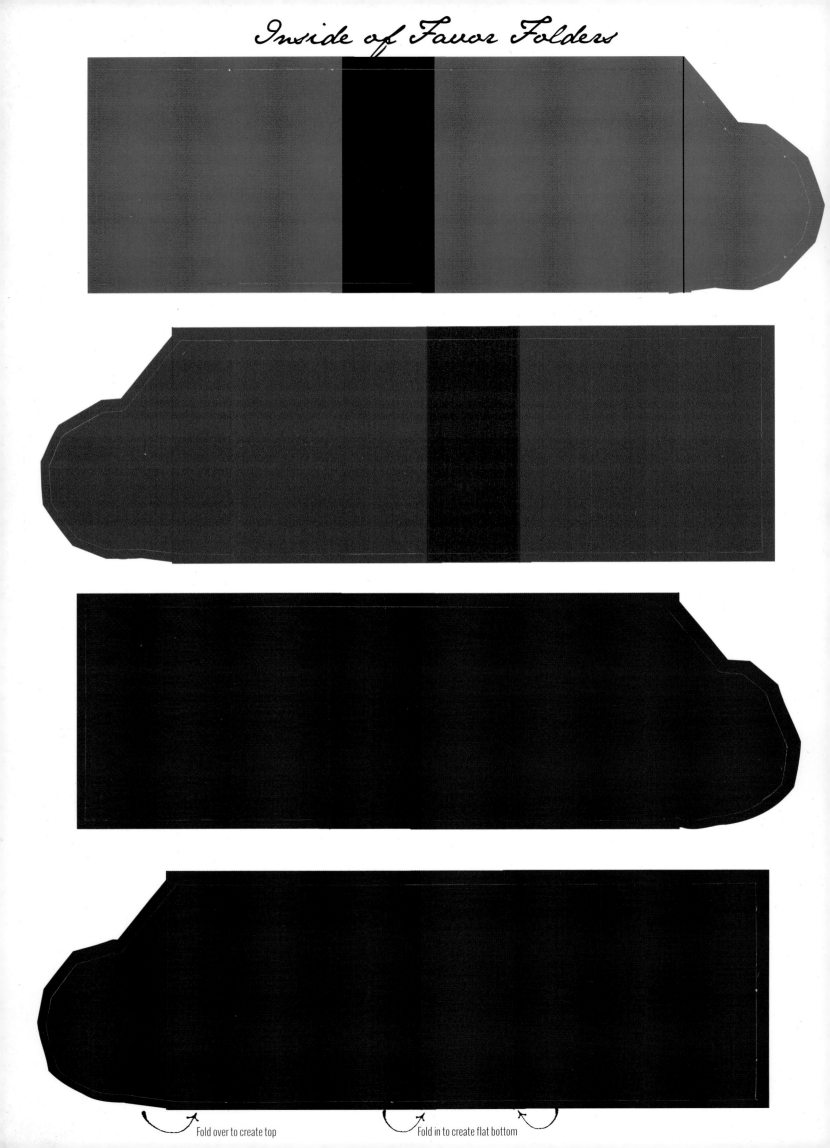

Fold over to create top   Fold in to create flat bottom

Coasters

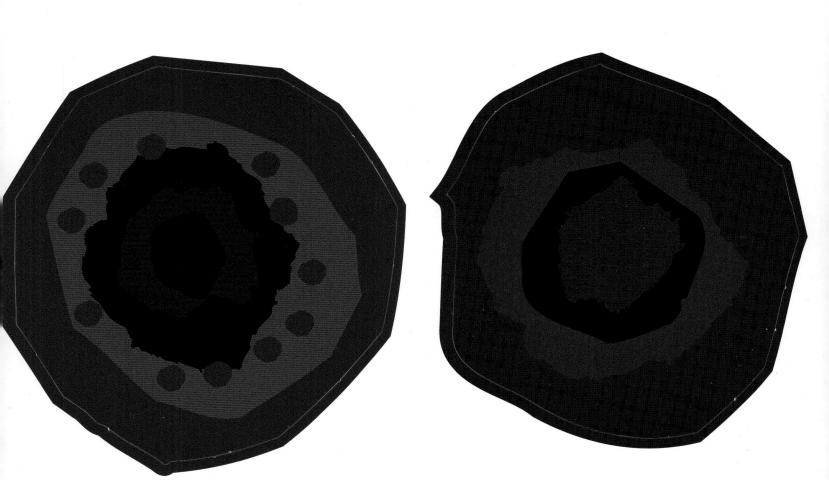

Coasters

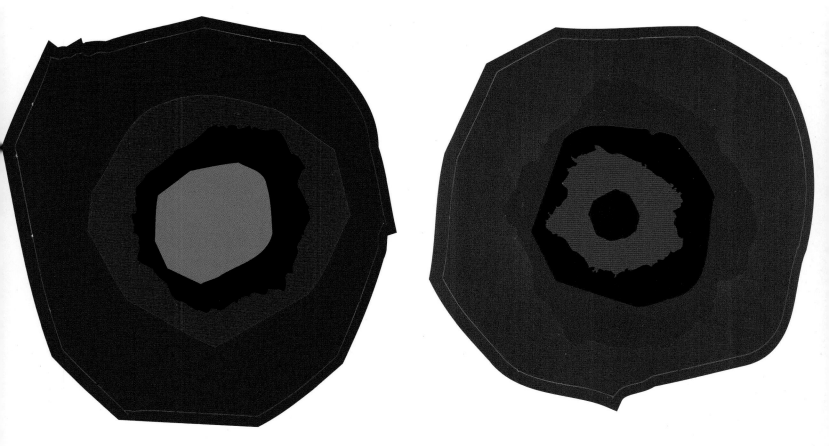

Coasters can also be used for decoration and embellishment
on just about everything in this book!
Hats, crowns, gifts, trays ...

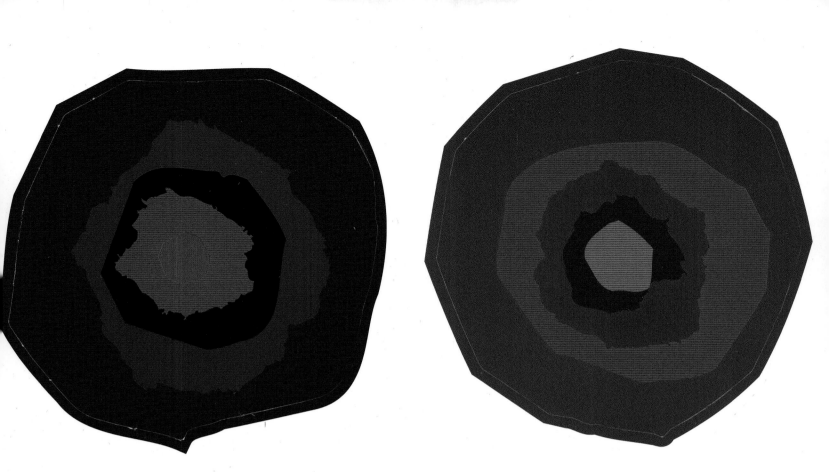

Coasters

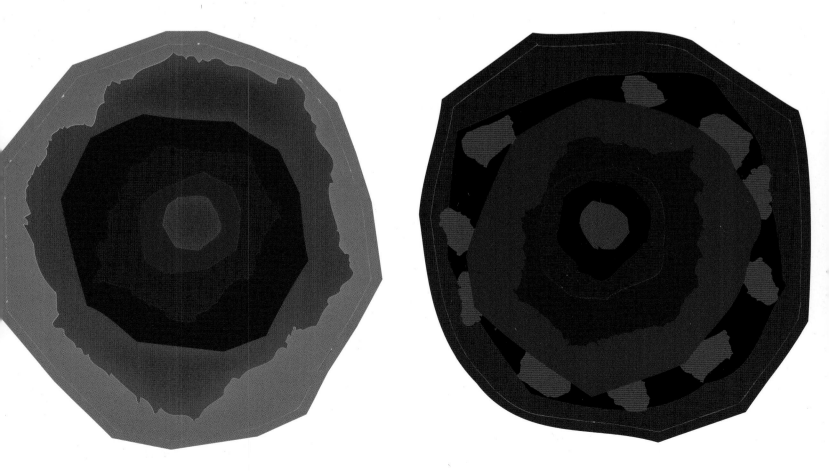

For longer lasting coasters, try laminating them.

Cupcakes

Cupcake Toppers

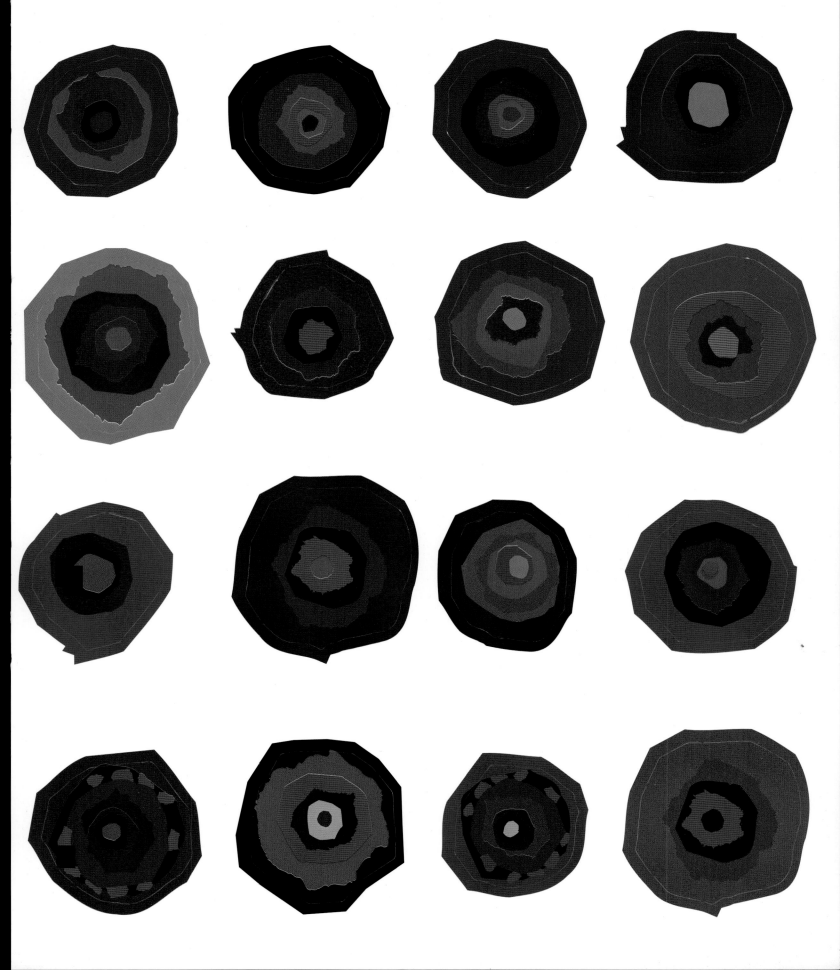

Match corresponding fronts and back, then glue to attach to toothpick or skewers for food decoration, cupcakes, cakes, sandwiches, or small bites. If used as garland, glue matching sides for double sided garland. Can be mixed with other garland squares or used alone as embellishment for any purpose. Combine with other shapes to decorate snack holders, crowns, hats, gifts, etc.

Cupcake Topper Backs

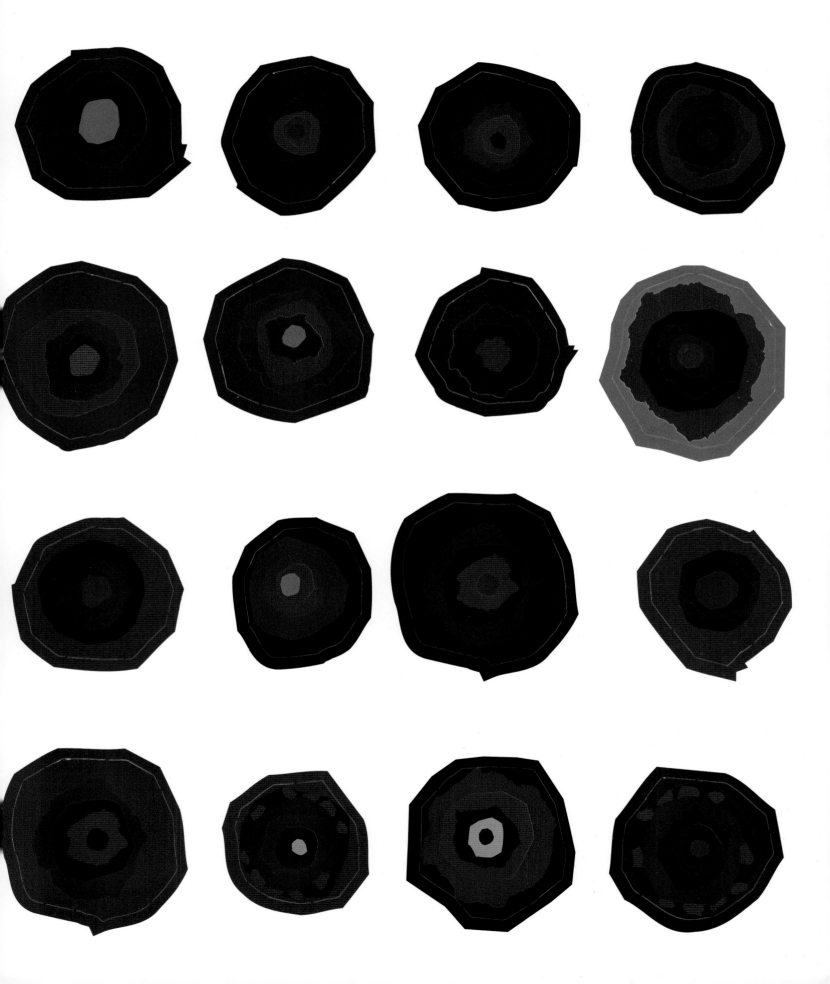

Match corresponding fronts and back, then glue to attach to toothpick or skewers for food decoration, cupcakes, cakes, sandwiches, or small bites. If used as garland, glue matching sides for double sided garland. Can be mixed with other garland squares or used alone as embellishment for any purpose. Combine with other shapes to decorate snack holders, crowns, hats, gifts, etc.

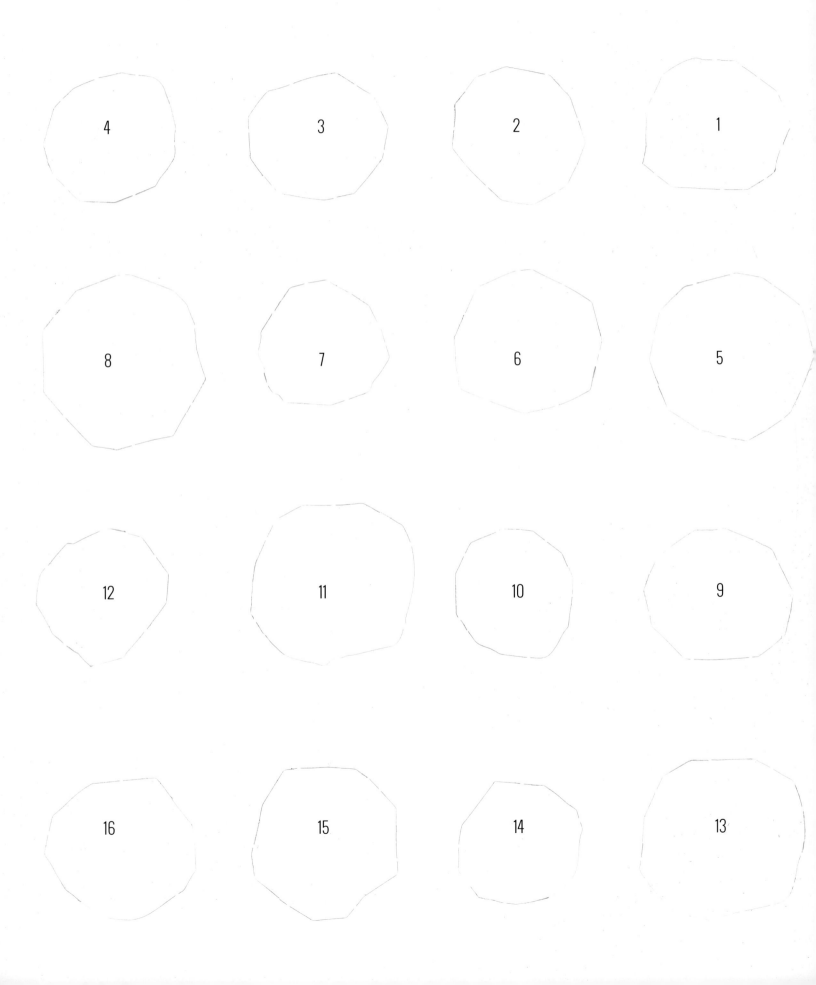

Cupcake Wrappers

Reverse print side.
Can be wrapped either side on cupcakes or cups.

Cupcakes come in many different
sizes, you may need to trim this
wrapper to fit.

Simply wrap around the cupcake to
measure, then secure at the tab with
tape or glue, which should be on the
inside to be invisible.

If you use them on solo or other dis-
posable cups, we suggest you secure
them all the way around the inside
with double-sided tape
to avoid slippage.

Reverse print side.
Can be wrapped either side on cupcakes or cups.

Cupcakes come in many different
sizes, you may need to trim this
wrapper to fit.

Simply wrap around the cupcake to
measure, then secure at the tab with
tape or glue, which should be on the
inside to be invisible.

If you use them on solo or other dis-
posable cups, we suggest you secure
them all the way around the inside
with double-sided tape
to avoid slippage.

Cupcake Wrappers

Reverse print side.
Can be wrapped either side on cupcakes or cups.

Cupcakes come in many different
sizes, you may need to trim this
wrapper to fit.

Simply wrap around the cupcake to
measure, then secure at the tab with
tape or glue, which should be on the
inside to be invisible.

If you use them on solo or other dis-
posable cups, we suggest you secure
them all the way around the inside
with double-sided tape
to avoid slippage.

Cupcake Wrappers

Reverse print side.
Can be wrapped either side on cupcakes or cups.

Cupcakes come in many different
sizes, you may need to trim this
wrapper to fit.

Simply wrap around the cupcake to
measure, then secure at the tab with
tape or glue, which should be on the
inside to be invisible.

If you use them on solo or other dis-
posable cups, we suggest you secure
them all the way around the inside
with double-sided tape
to avoid slippage.

Dots and striped blocks can create several garlands, mix or match. They can also seal bags embellish gift wrap, or label food.

Garland

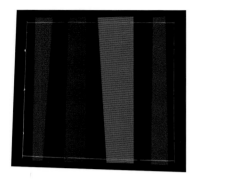
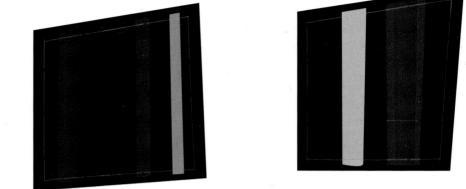
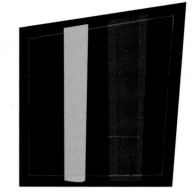
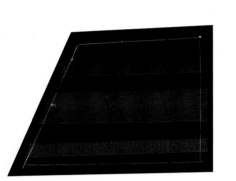
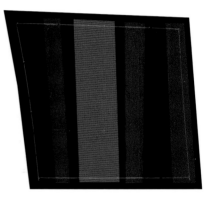
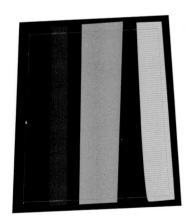

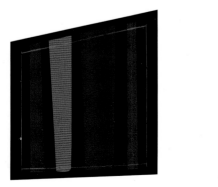
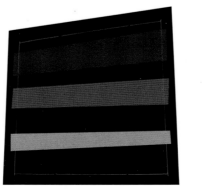
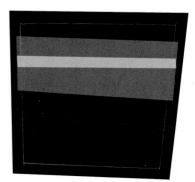

Match corresponding fronts and back, then glue to attach to toothpick or skewers for food decoration, cupcakes, cakes, sandwiches, or small bites. If used as garland, glue matching sides for double-sided garland. Can be mixed with other garland squares or used alone as embellishment for any purpose.
Combine with other shapes to decorate snack holders, crowns, hats, gifts, etc.

Or tags, seals, decoration

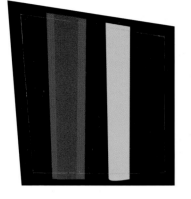

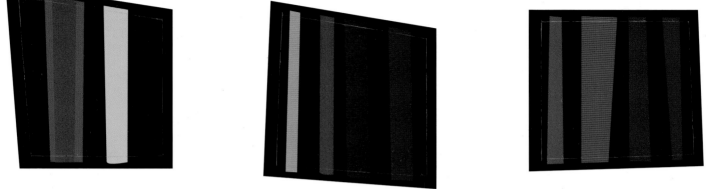

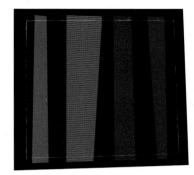

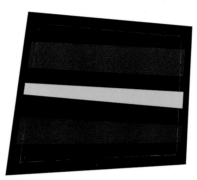

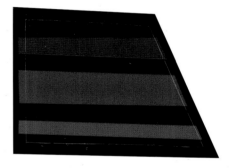

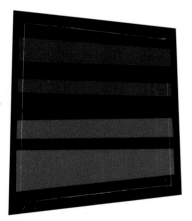

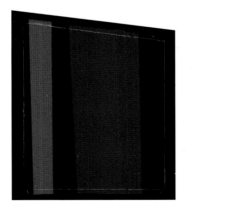

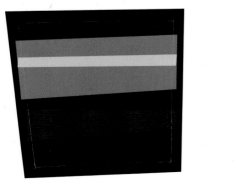

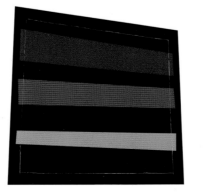

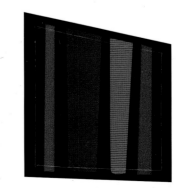

Match corresponding fronts and back, then glue to attach to toothpick or skewers for food decoration, cupcakes, cakes, sandwiches, or small bites. If used as garland, glue matching sides for double-sided garland. Can be mixed with other garland squares or used alone as embellishment for any purpose.
Combine with other shapes to decorate snack holders, crowns, hats, gifts, etc.

More garland

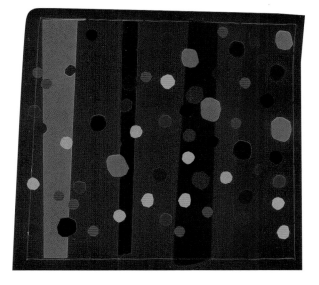
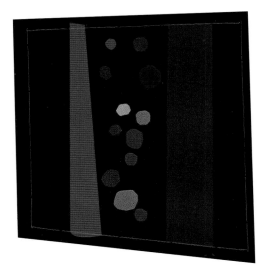
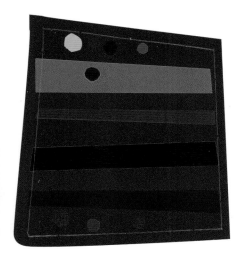
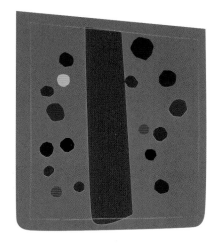
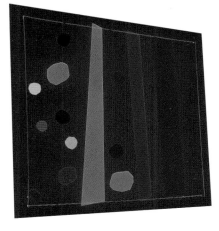
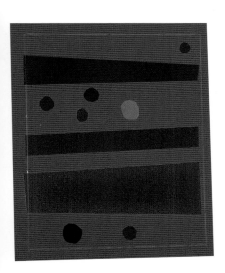
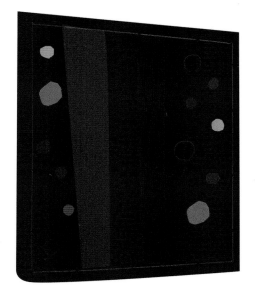
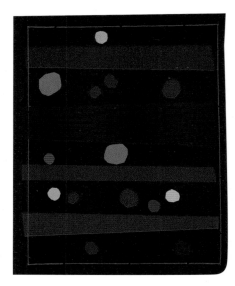

Match corresponding fronts and back, then glue to attach to toothpick or skewers for food decoration, cupcakes, cakes, sandwiches, or small bites. If used as garland, glue matching sides for double-sided garland. Can be mixed with other garland squares or used alone as embellishment for any purpose.
Combine with other shapes to decorate snack holders, crowns, hats, gifts, etc.

More garland

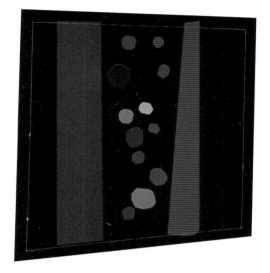

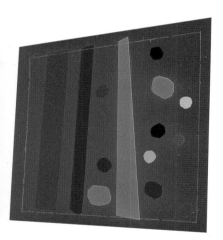
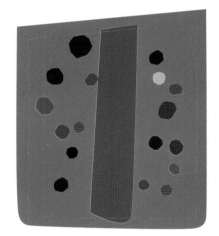

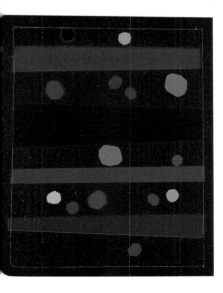
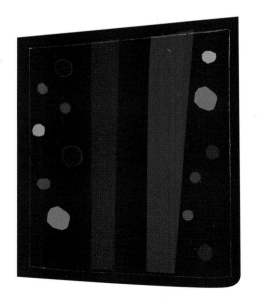
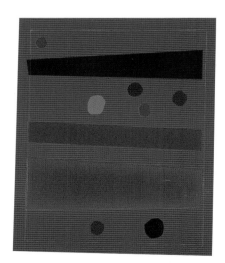

Match corresponding fronts and back, then glue to attach to toothpick or skewers for food decoration, cupcakes, cakes, sandwiches, or small bites. If used as garland, glue matching sides for double-sided garland. Can be mixed with other garland squares or used alone as embellishment for any purpose.
Combine with other shapes to decorate snack holders, crowns, hats, gifts, etc.

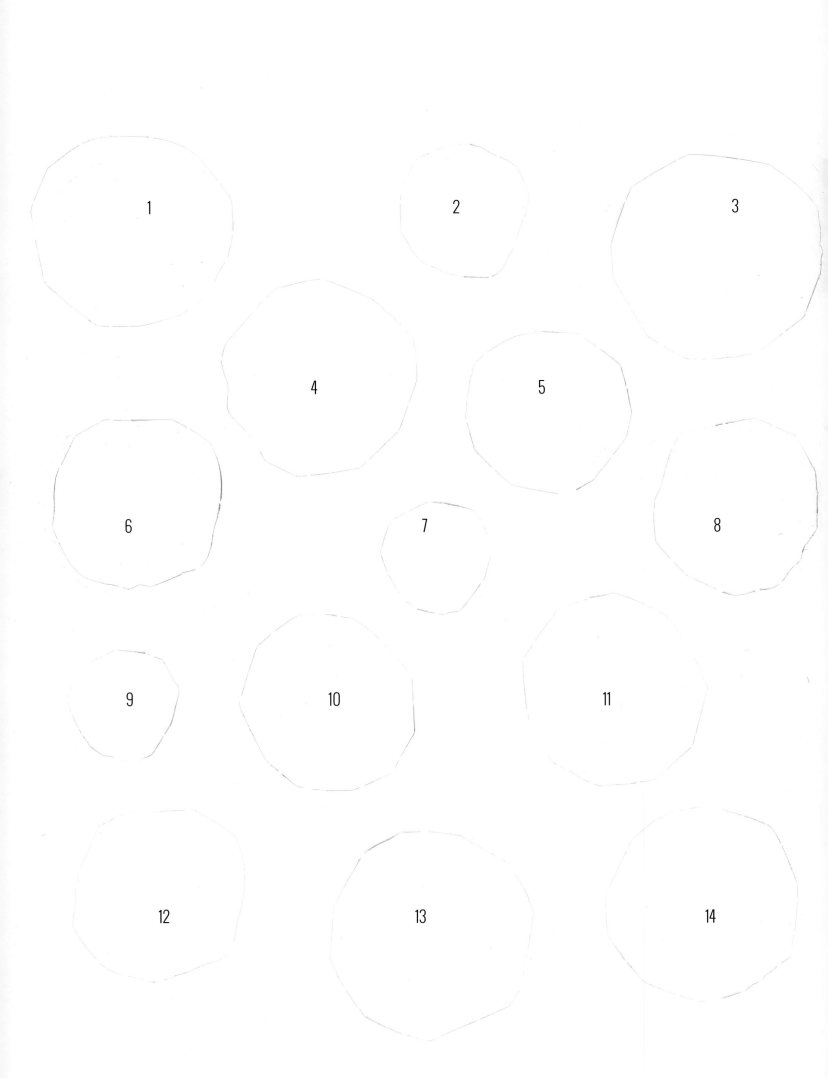

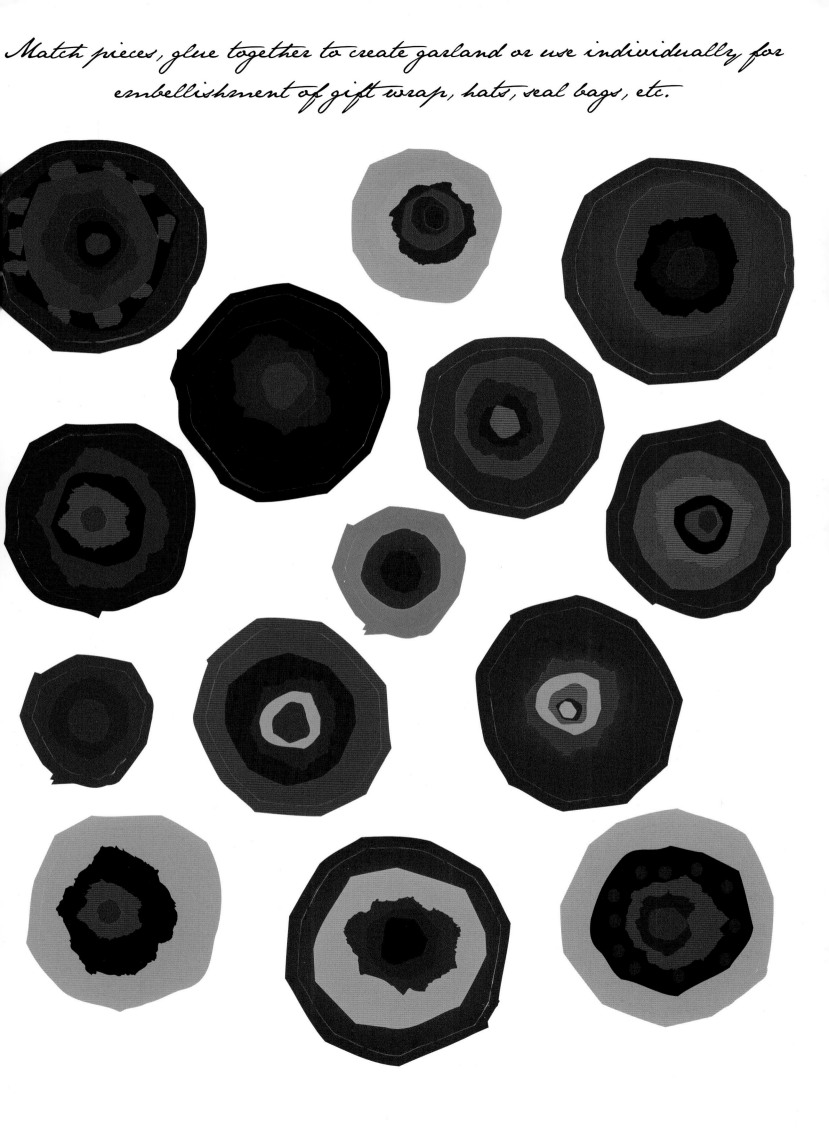

Match pieces, glue together to create garland or use individually, for embellishment of gift wrap, hats, seal bags, etc.

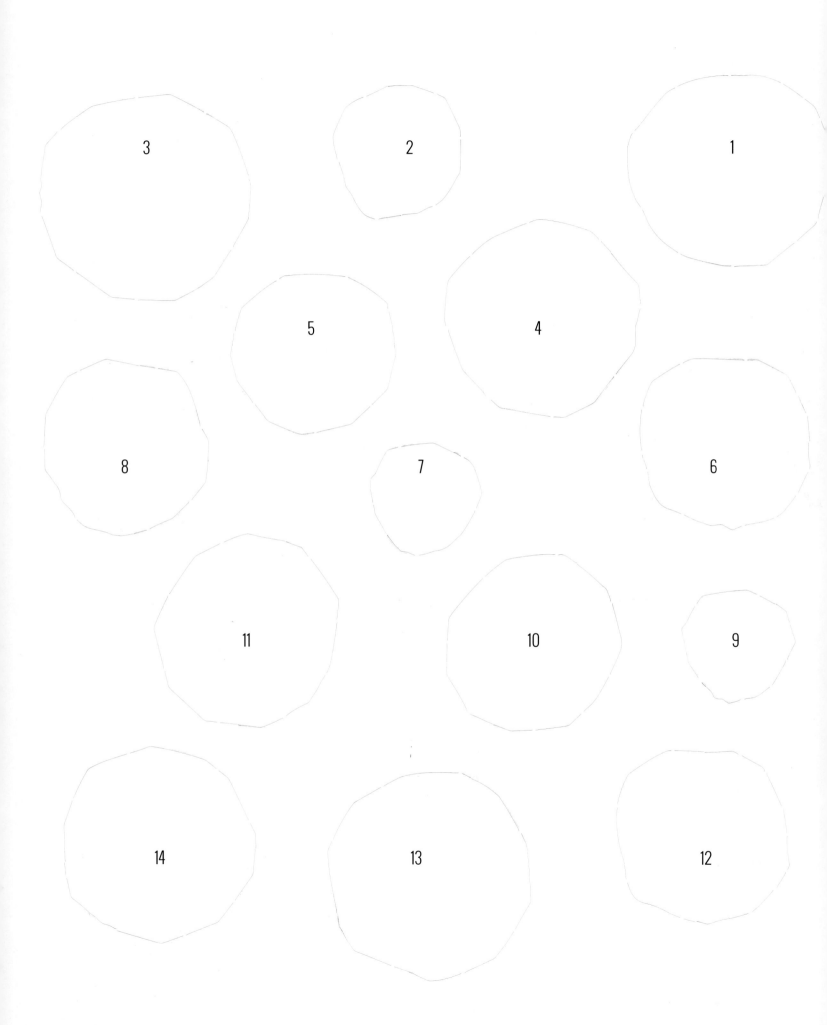

Garland, embellishment, tags

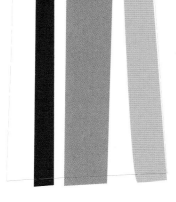

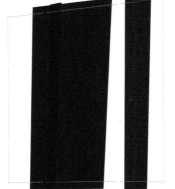

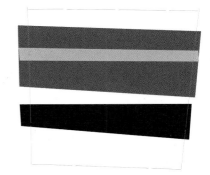

Match pieces, glue together to create garland or use individually for
embellishment of gift wrap, hats, seal bags, etc.

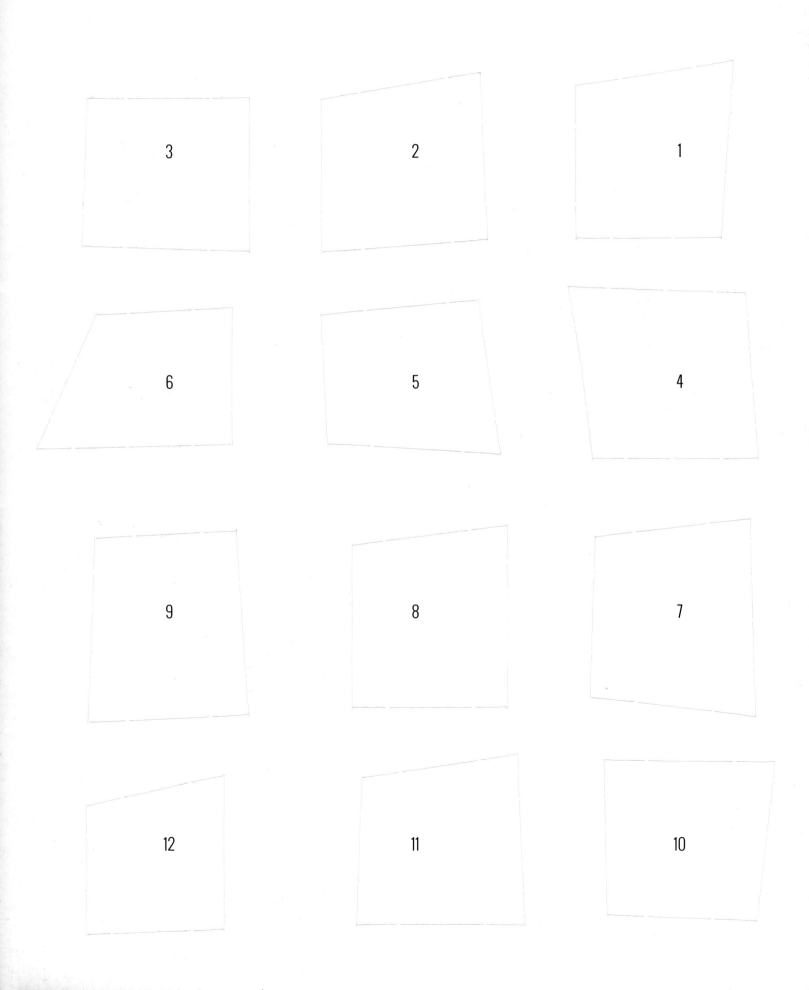

Labels

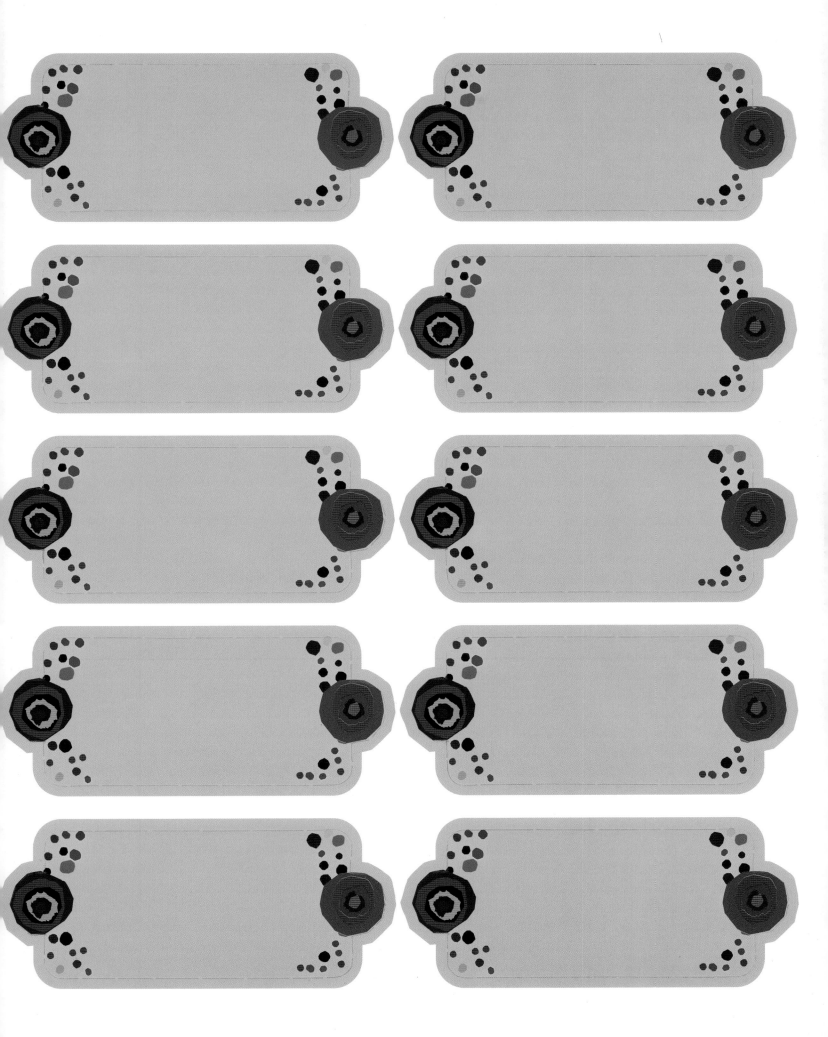

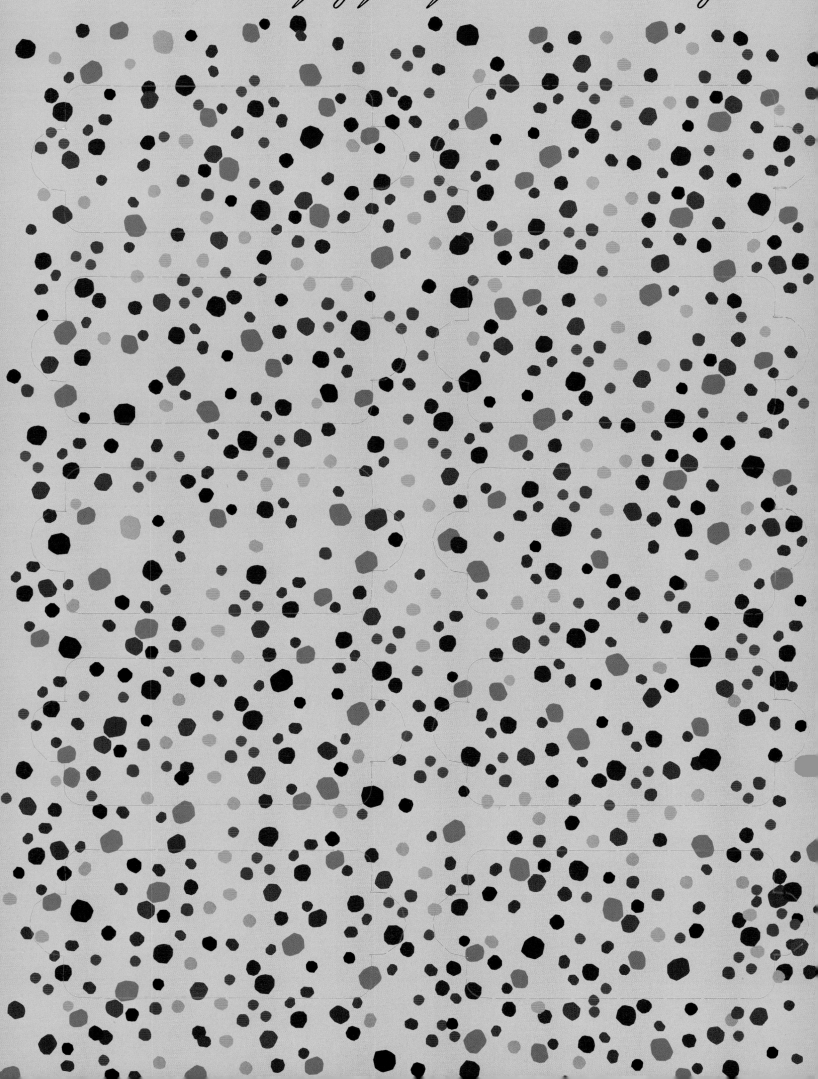

Use these labels for gifts or food or even as name tags

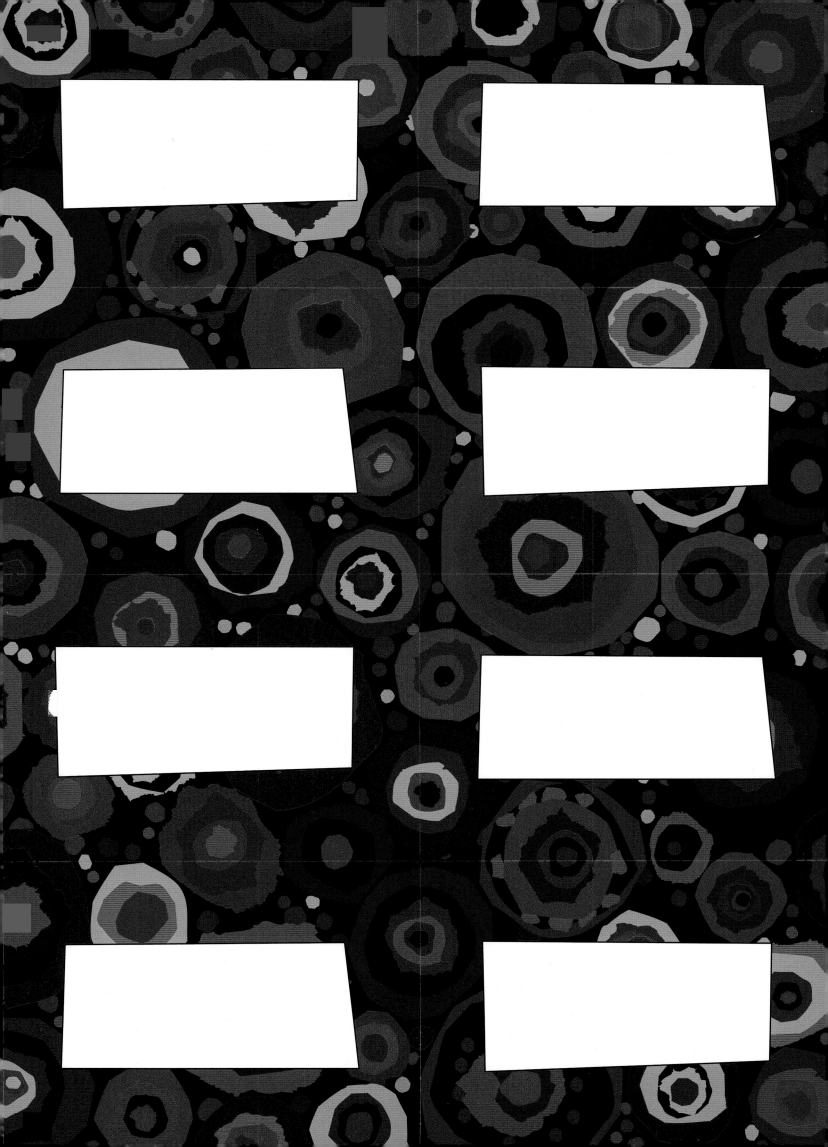

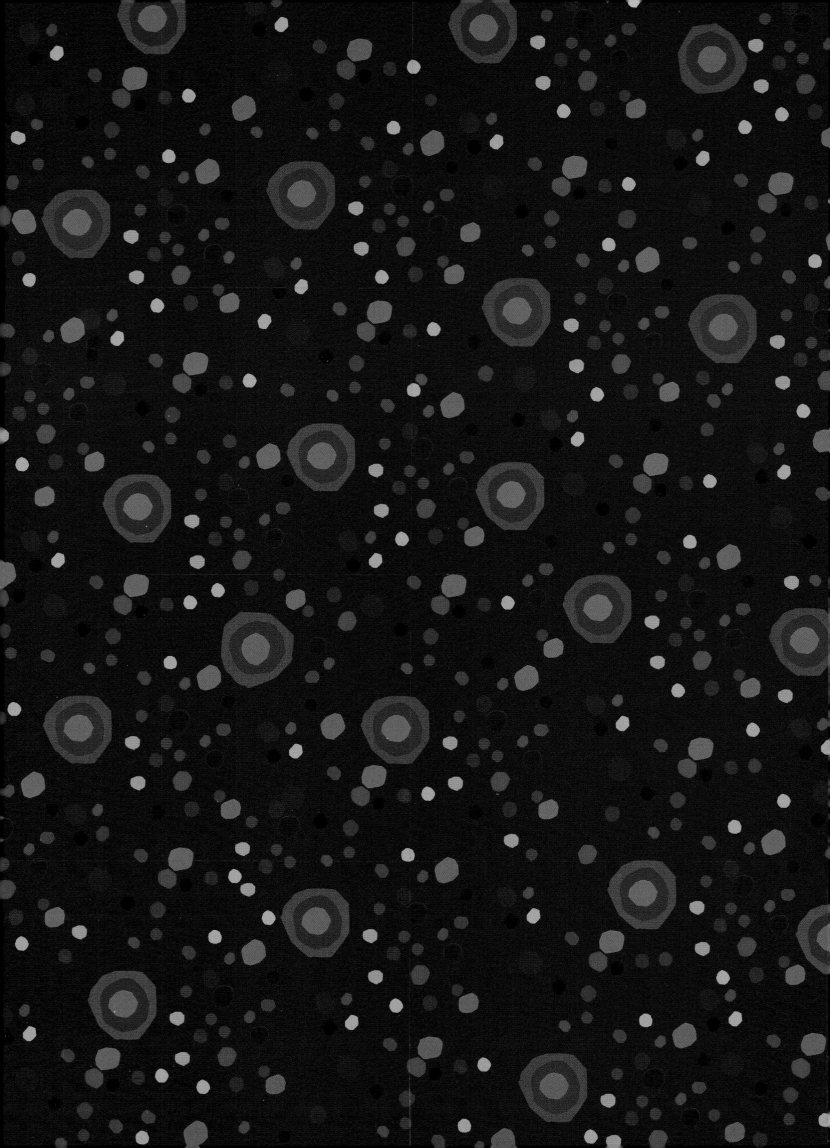

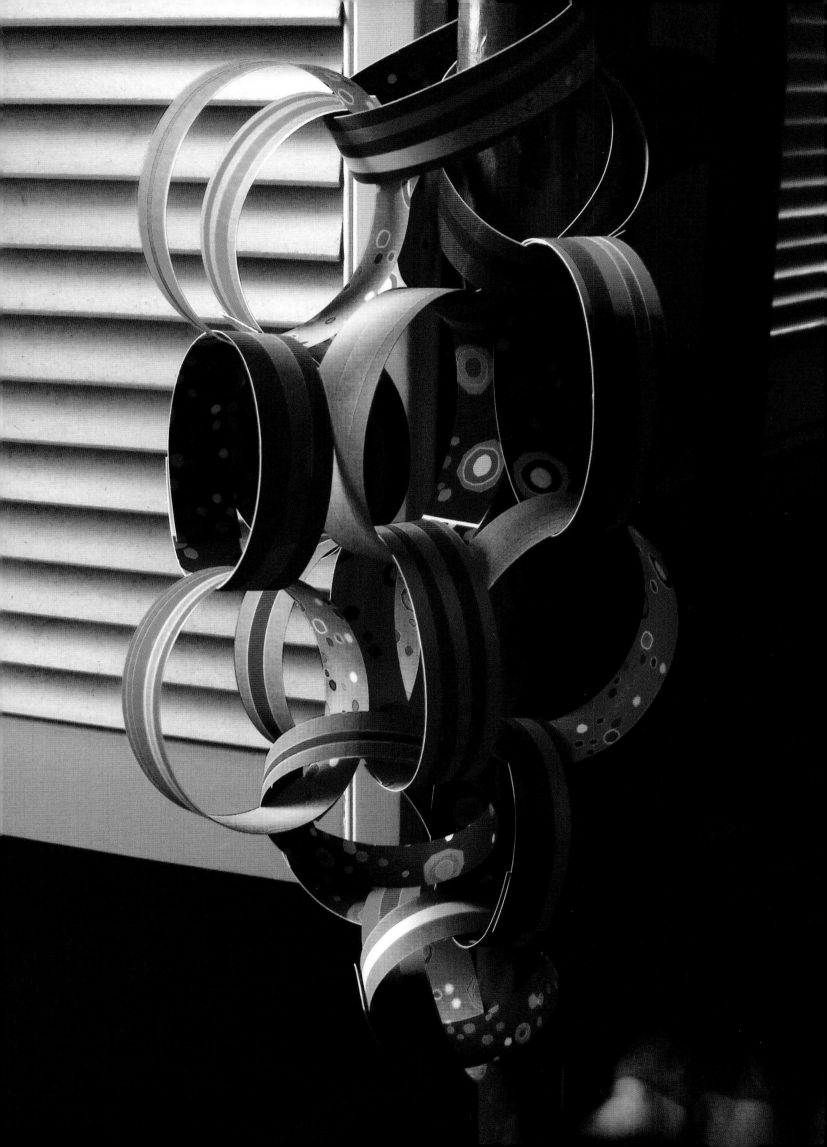

Chain
Garland
Strips

MUSHROOM BRIE

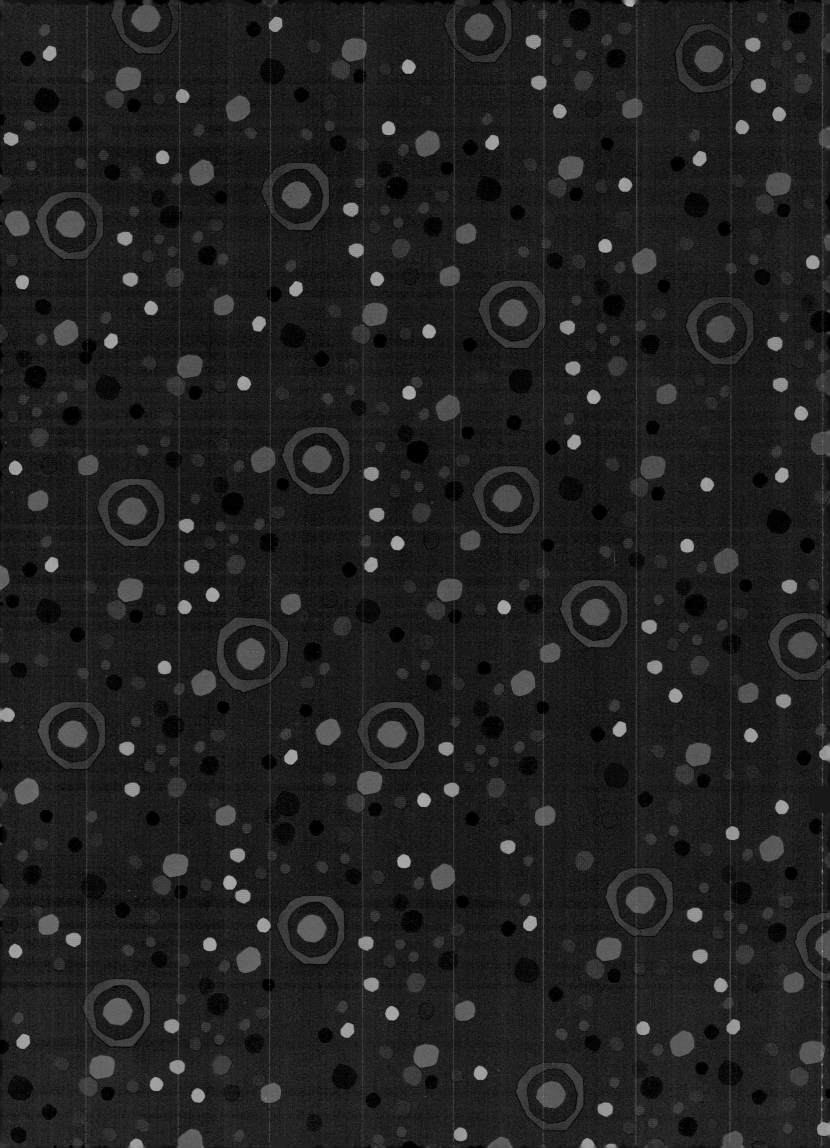

Tray Liners

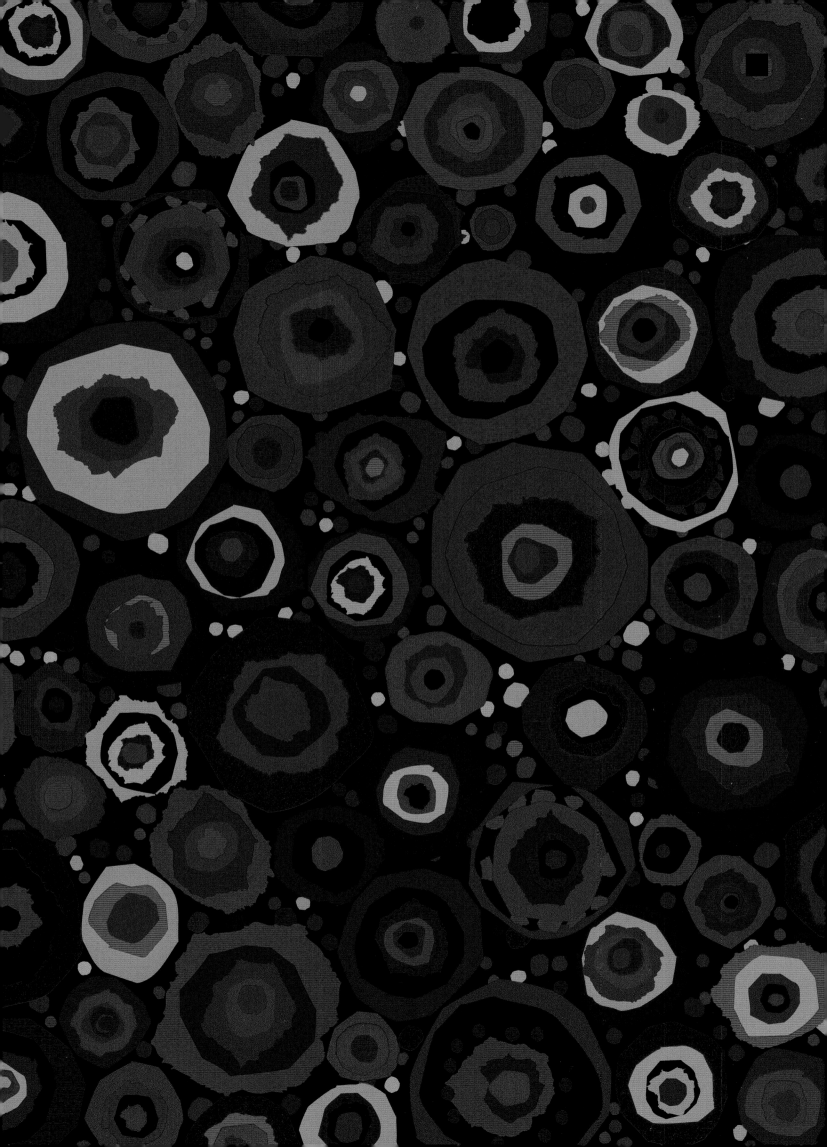

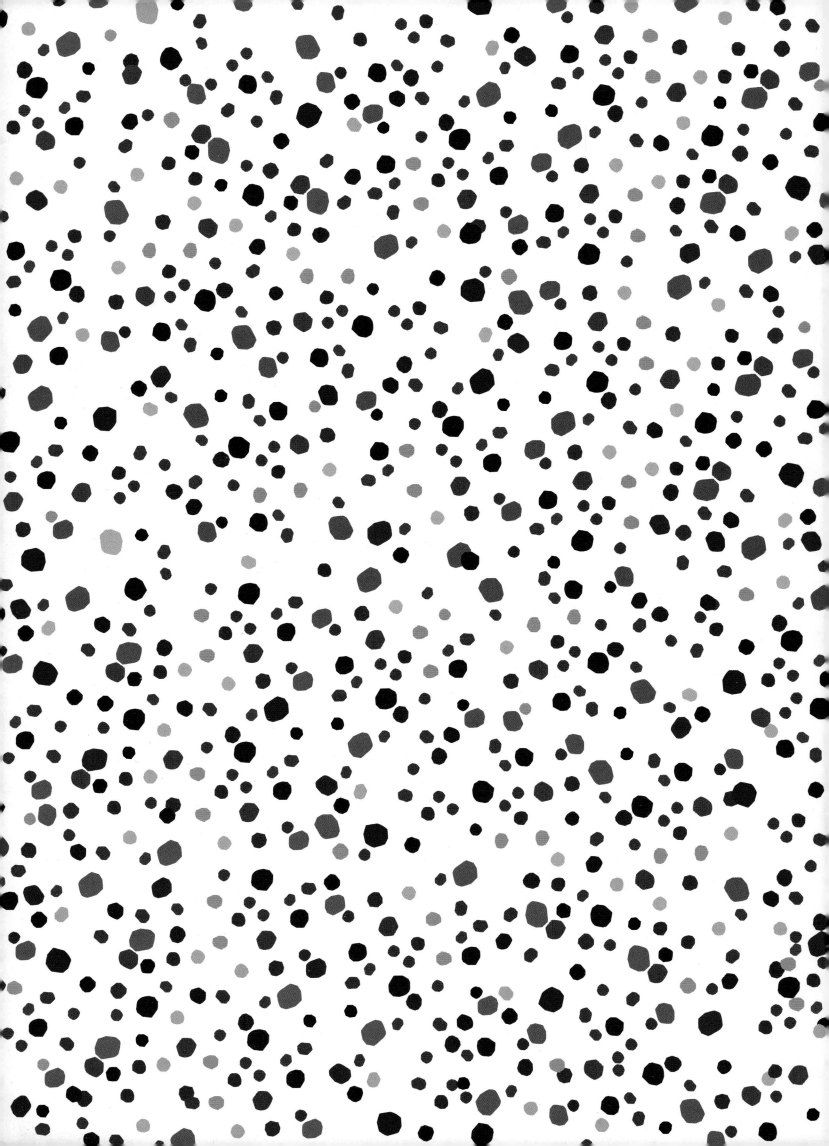

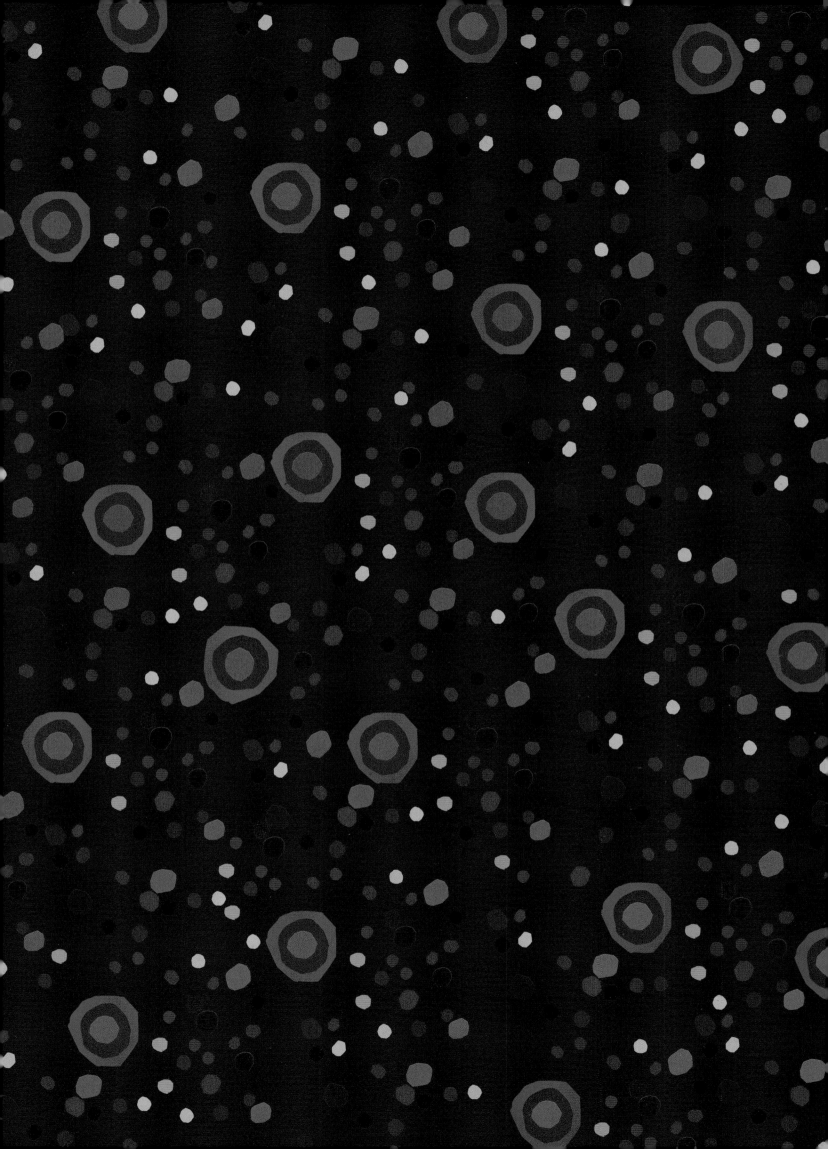

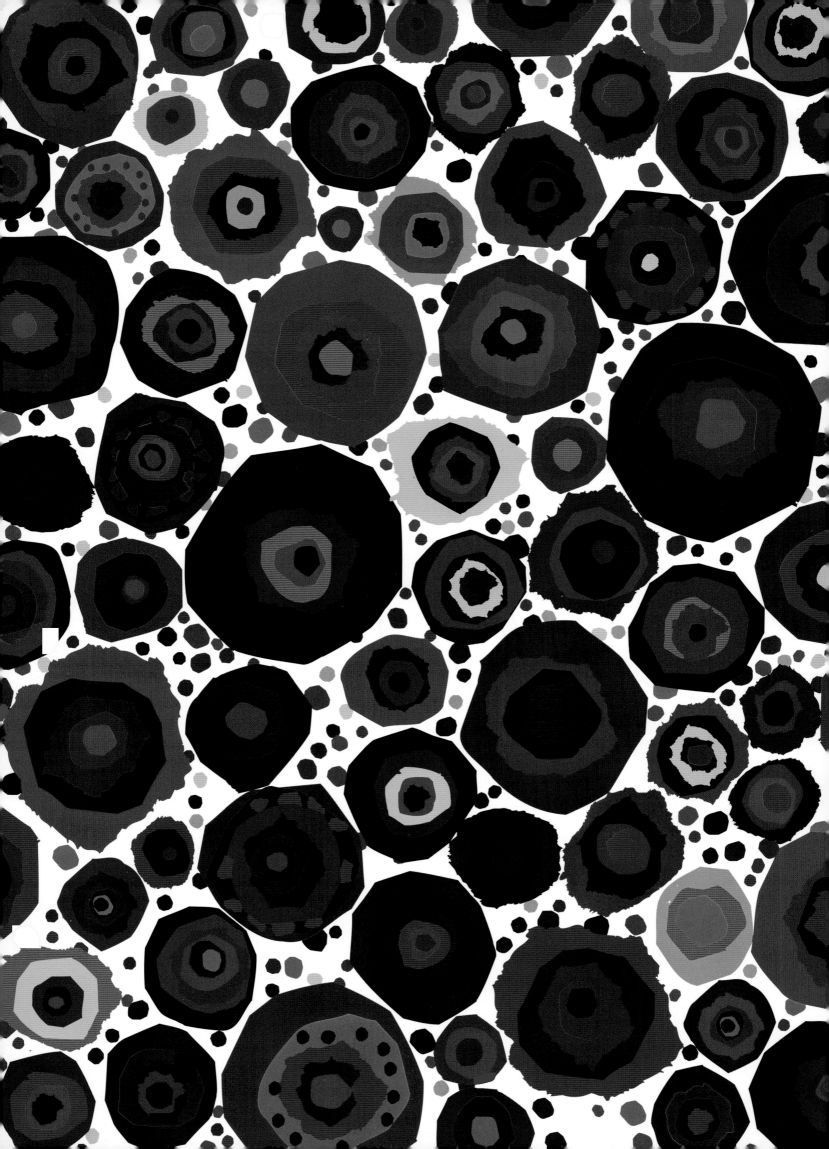

To roll the cones, hold like this and tape or glue the tab to the inside, which ever pattern you choose for the inside, spots or stripes.

To make a basket, simply attach one of the garland strips to both sides of the opening. To use the cones for hats, a bit of elastic thread or yarn will hold the hat on. Ribbon tends to slip.

To use a coaster for flowers or hats, cut a thin "V" in the edge toward the center, bring the edges together and tape or glue. This will make them three-dimensional.

To wrap a cupcake or a solo cup, simply choose a side and wrap until the tab overlaps and secure with tape or glue. Cupcakes come in many sizes, these wraps are on the large side. You may need to trim to fit with scissors.

To fold the snack holders fold the side in a the points until you have four tabs. If you choose to, you can crease the bottom. Now bring the back and front together and tape or glue at the sides. Front folds over the back, so that the seam is on the inside.

Fold the favor folders along the solid shape color blocks, fold over the top. You can write a note inside or just tuck a treat into the folder. You may want to secure the treat - fold the spot over the top and secure with a bit of tape or glue. If you crease it well, you may not need to seal the folder so it can be reused.

To make a tray with the tray liners, simply slip the side you choose face up into a picture frame.

Box or shadow frames work well, but any frame will do as long as it can be secured at the back. For vintage frames reinforce the backing to avoid slippage. For a larger tray you can use a frame with a mat. Or you can trim to fit a smaller frame.

These double sided sheets can be used multiple times. For use in serving food directly on the papers you can apply clear contact paper or laminate to avoid wilting.

Photo credit © 2014 Rebecca Emberley
Photo credit pages 36 tl, 36 bl, 41, 73 b © 2014 Rainer Schwake

First Edition December 2014
Published by Two Little Birds Books
www.twolittlebirdsbooks.com
Distributed by AMMO Books
Printed in Malaysia
ISBN: 978-0-9912935-4-4
Library of Congress Control #: 2014915402

The fonts used in the book are Jane Austen, Black Olives and Oswald Light.

For Adrian - always a party inspiration.

For all the paper geeks like me who don't always have the time to start from scratch.

And for everyone who helped and encouraged this project -
Peter, Rainer, Susan, Susannah, Paula, Gwen, Elizabeth, Nina, Ann and of course my parents, Ed & Barbara, who set me on the path to this book many years ago.

And special thanks to our models Tula, Adrian, Saorsie and Chloe!